*Remembering*

# University of Michigan Football

### Michelle O'Brien

## TURNER
PUBLISHING COMPANY

Michigan kicks off to Minnesota to start the Wolverines' homecoming game of 1910. Michigan was victorious, 6–0, and thus kept the earthenware water jug—the trophy known as the "Little Brown Jug"—they had won back from Minnesota the previous year.

*Remembering*

# University of Michigan Football

Turner Publishing Company
4507 Charlotte Avenue • Suite 100
Nashville, Tennessee 37209
(615) 255-2665

*Remembering University of Michigan Football*

www.turnerpublishing.com

Library of Congress Control Number: 2010926214

ISBN: 978-1-59652-690-7
ISBN-13: 978-168336-900-4 (pbk)

Printed in the United States of America

# CONTENTS

Seen here in 1926, his last season as Michigan's head coach, Fielding Yost, at far left, holds the attention of his assistants, including several former University of Michigan players who themselves had turned to coaching—Elton Wieman, kneeling at immediate right of Yost; Harry Kipke, in the white shirt; and Jack Blott, kneeling at left of Kipke. Wieman and Kipke would become head coaches at Michigan.

# Acknowledgments

This volume, *Remembering University of Michigan Football,* is the result of the cooperation and efforts of many individuals and organizations. It is with great thanks that we acknowledge the valuable contribution of the Bentley Historical Library, University of Michigan, for its generous support.

We would also like to thank the following individuals for valuable contributions and assistance in making this work possible:

Dr. Mark Looker

James O'Brien

With the exception of cropping images where needed and touching up imperfections that have accrued over time, no changes have been made to the photographs in this volume. The caliber and clarity of many photographs are limited by the technology of the day and the ability of the photographer at the time they were made.

# PREFACE

The photographs in this collection follow the University of Michigan football program from its birth through the first hundred years of its history. With inspirational coaches leading the Michigan Wolverines through countless battles on the gridiron, and with players giving it their all while fighting for victory in a growing sport, the early teams represented something greater than themselves: the University of Michigan, the first school west of Pennsylvania to establish a football team.

As the university grew and the world changed, so too did the football program, persisting through social and political upheaval. While the Depression brought turmoil to most of the United States, the program continued, providing opportunities for young men to work and learn. Many former players were among the valiant young soldiers who fought in the two world wars; several returned to play again at Michigan.

After World War II, the increasing complexity of the game and its heightened popularity created new possibilities for players and more excitement for fans. Students bustled around campus in anticipation of each Saturday match. Then as now, the colors maize and blue lived not only through the players who wore the Michigan jersey and donned the winged helmet but through all those who cheered for the Wolverines each season. Whether in victory or defeat, the Michigan football team carried the pride of the university onto the field every game.

A variety of stages have showcased Michigan football over the decades. The first on-campus field, Regents, was maintained by the student association, and all of Michigan's outdoor athletics were played on this single field. As time went on and the football program grew with the rest of the university, expansion became necessary, so the land for Ferry Field was donated to the school. The Wolverines played at Ferry Field until there were more Michigan fans than seats. When the school approved the building of the "Big House," Michigan Stadium, coach and athletic director Fielding Yost made sure the design allowed for future expansion. Just as he had anticipated, Michigan fans flocked to the new facility in ever increasing numbers.

But it didn't stop there. A new stage—television—brought Michigan football to an even wider audience beginning with the first televised game in the 1940s. From that point on, Michigan fans throughout the nation could join in the spirit of watching and cheering the Wolverines in their gridiron clashes at the Big House and elsewhere.

Michigan has spawned many football legends, from its first Heisman Trophy winner to assorted record-breakers and memorable left-handed quarterbacks. The Wolverines were the first team to travel to California to play in the Tournament of Roses game, now the Rose Bowl. The team has inspired and triumphed under great songs such as "The Victors" and "Yellow and Blue," and although Michigan football has only retired five jersey numbers, it has produced countless All-Americans and a host of professional players.

Beginning with the first team in 1879, Michigan football became an integral part of campus life, its impact spreading far beyond the field. To this day alumni come back in huge numbers to cheer their alma mater, even as great players sometimes return to coach the Maize and Blue. The spirit that is Michigan football never leaves its fans.

—*Michelle O'Brien*

This aerial view shows the newly built Michigan Stadium at full capacity for the stadium dedication game in 1927.

# The Beginnings of Michigan Football

## (1879–1926)

The 1879 University of Michigan football team, seen here, may have played only two games its first season and had no coach, but it became the first university west of Pennsylvania to form a team. Michigan played and won its first intercollegiate football game, against Racine College at White Stockings Park in Chicago, on May 30 that year.

Michigan faced Cornell twice in November 1894. The Wolverines lost 22–0 in the first meeting; but three weeks later, playing here at the Detroit Athletic Club Field with a home crowd cheering them on, Michigan defeated Cornell 12–4 and would finish the season with a record of 9-1-1.

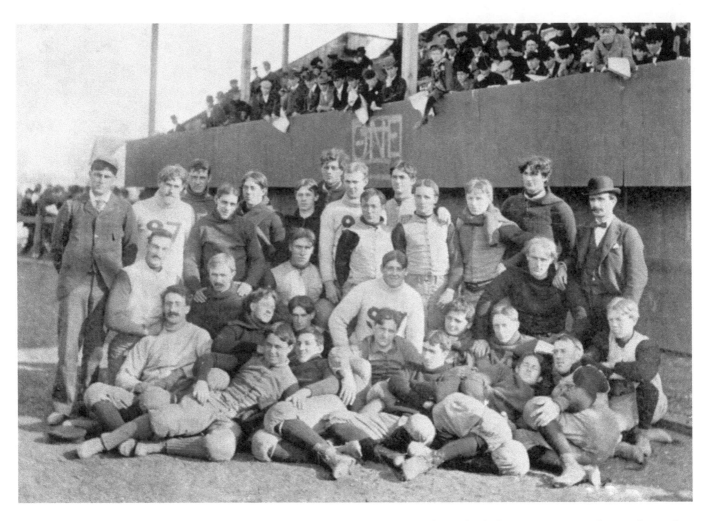

Following the outstanding season of the year before, the 1895 University of Michigan football team seen posing here in front of the Regents Field grandstand would only lose one game, to Harvard, 4–0. The 1895 team was led by captain Frederick Henninger, kneeling three from left in the third row, and quarterback James Baird, directly behind Henninger. Baird, notably, figured out he could pass a ball more quickly if he received it from center while standing instead of kneeling.

In 1897, after it was ruled that only former students could become coaches at the university, the Student-Alumni Advisory Board elected Gustave Ferbert, at far right, to take over from William Ward. Ferbert had played halfback for Michigan in 1894-96. The fifth coach at the university, he became the first to win the conference title, in 1898. Helping him coach, as seen here left to right, were Ferbert's former teammates William Malley, Thad Farnham, and Giovanni Villa, and an unidentified fourth assistant.

As early as the 1890s, the University of Michigan football team had its own designated official shoemakers, seen here at work in their shop.

Established in 1896, the University of Michigan Band was led initially by a student director, Eugene Fischer. Seen here in its 1897 incarnation, the band would play at its first football game in the fall of 1898.

Under the direction of new coach Fielding H. Yost, the 1901 Michigan team seen here finished the regular season with a record of 10-0, tying Wisconsin for the conference title, and defeated Stanford in the first ever Tournament of Roses game, later known as the Rose Bowl. Having outscored its opponents by more than 500 points total on the season, including a 128–0 defeat of Buffalo, the 1901 squad earned the nickname "Point-a-Minute."

The 1901 University of Michigan team rides in the Rose Parade. This was the first trip to the West Coast for many of the players. The parade colors that year were blue and yellow, which led many Stanford fans to believe themselves outnumbered in the stands. Michigan's victory solidified its prominent place in football.

Regents Field was established in 1893. Michigan's football team played on this field—purchased by the regents to provide students with their own on-campus sports site—until 1905.

The 1902 Wolverines set up in "tackle back" formation, one of Yost's innovations. The coach was famous for motivational sayings addressed to his team such as "It's the thing you work the hardest for that means the most to you."

At Regents Field in 1902, the University of Michigan captain, Boss Weeks, prepares to tackle an Ohio State ball carrier for a five-yard loss. Michigan's "Point-a-Minute" team dominated Ohio State by outscoring them 214–6 during the years 1901-5.

The action is heavy in 1903 at Regents Field. Michigan won every game it played at Regents that year.

Although Michigan beat Drake University 47–0 in this 1903 meeting, the game was a challenge for the Wolverines. It was one of the hardest-fought games of the season. Drake kept the Wolverines to only short carries in the first half. Finally, in the second half, Michigan was able to penetrate Drake's defense, scoring five touchdowns in the last 26 minutes of play.

Willie Heston carries the ball for Michigan against Wisconsin in 1903. Heston was an All-American halfback. With the yards he gained against Wisconsin, and with Tom Hammond's accurate placekicks accounting for 10 points, the Wolverines won the game 16–0.

Walter Camp and Fielding Yost meet at the 1903 Michigan-Chicago game. Fielding "Hurry-Up" Yost was the first Michigan coach to win a national title, and his undefeated streak begun in 1901 continued through the 1903 season and beyond. Walter Camp is considered the "Father of American Football." In 1880 he proposed changes to the rules of the game that would prove definitive, such as establishing the line of scrimmage and the snap, and reducing the number of players on the field for each side from 15 to 11.

Despite the blizzard conditions on Thanksgiving Day 1903 at Chicago's Marshall Field, 20,000 frozen Chicago fans watched the game, hoping that Michigan's well-oiled machine could be stopped. But not even the conditions could slow the Wolverines down, as seen here with Michigan quarterback John Henry "Harry" James handing the ball to Willie Heston en route to a 28–0 victory.

Composer Louis Elbel, seen in the corner photo inset of this sheet music cover, was inspired to write "The Victors" after the 1898 Michigan squad beat Chicago 12–11. Having celebrated in the streets of Chicago with other Michigan fans, he realized they did not have an appropriate celebration song. So on the long train ride back to Ann Arbor, Elbel wrote "The Victors," which has become one of college football's most recognized fight songs.

The 1904 football team sits in a carriage in front of University Hall. The players are wearing their new Michigan sweaters displaying a solid block "M" on the chest.

The university's football training table seen here is where the players ate meals together during the season. The arrangement encouraged players to get to know one another so they could play more closely as a unit on the field. Sitting in front on the left side are Ted Stuart, Fred Norcross, Harry Hammond, and William Clark. On the opposite side of the table are Thomas Hammond, Henry Schulte, and Walter Graham.

The University of Chicago ventured to Regents Field in 1904 for the last game of the season, with Michigan still undefeated. Here Tom Hammond, a Michigan end like his brother Harry (both originally from Chicago), carries the ball into the clear for the Wolverines. Winning 22–12, Michigan finished its season undefeated.

Michigan's offense practices the handoff. The 1905 team gained much of its yardage rushing the ball.

The teams line up for the opening kickoff of the Wisconsin-Michigan game at Regents Field in 1905, the last game played at Regents. Due to the success of Yost's teams of 1901-5, interest in Michigan football skyrocketed and a new stadium was needed. With construction almost done on Ferry Field, the Wolverines said good-bye to Regents before a crowd of 17,000.

Bricklayers stand in front of the finished north wall of Ferry Field, which was completed in time for the 1906 season. The need for more space for athletics had arisen in 1902, as more and more buildings had come to occupy the once vacant fields around Ann Arbor. To meet the university's needs, philanthropist Dexter Ferry bought and donated 20 acres of land for Michigan athletics. Ferry also provided funds for a brick wall and gates to adorn three sides of the field.

The Michigan team sits on the sidelines at the University of Pennsylvania's Franklin Field in 1906. Leading up to the game, Michigan had yet to lose that season, but Pennsylvania proved to be the better team, winning 17–0.

Michigan fans watch Pennsylvania take on their Wolverines. Fielding Yost is in the stands, in the hat at right of the three men sitting close together in the foreground.

Michigan scores a touchdown against Minnesota in the 1909 game.

The 1911 Michigan football team poses in and around an automobile.

Michigan kicks off to Cornell at Ferry Field in the last home game of 1912, which Michigan won 20–12. This was a major victory for the Wolverines, considering they had played Cornell six times since 1889 and had lost every single matchup until that day.

The famous "block M" fills the Michigan students' section during the 1916 game against Pennsylvania. Students would hold up pennants of either yellow or blue to create the M in support of their Wolverines on the field. They also sang "Yellow and Blue" during the Penn game, but Michigan lost.

A crowd numbered at 22,000 cheered on the Yellow and Blue (better known today as the Maize and Blue) in the 1915 homecoming game against Cornell. This time Michigan lost, 34–7. Cornell always posed a great challenge for Michigan.

Fullback Elton "Tad" Wieman carries the ball across "No Man's Land" in 1917. Wieman went on to serve as assistant coach at Michigan during the years 1921-26, and in 1927 he took over as head coach for two seasons after Yost.

Coach Fielding Yost, in the fedora, stands on the sidelines with his team at halftime of a game in 1918. The 1918 season was shortened due to the devastating influenza epidemic and to travel restrictions imposed because of World War I.

The 1923 edition of the University of Michigan Marching Band poses on the steps of the Rackham Building.

Michigan team captain Herb Steger pushes through the line during the 1924 game against the University of Illinois. His efforts in a game that Michigan would eventually lose had coaches encouraging players to "run like Steger."

Fans stand at the gates of Ferry Field to get a glimpse at the on-field action. By this time, as the Ferry Field era neared its close, Michigan football had earned a place in any discussion of the leading programs in college sports.

Fielding Yost stands smiling with Bennie Oosterbaan and Benny Friedman, his dynamic duo. Oosterbaan was considered one of the greatest receivers of his day and, along with quarterback Friedman, was named All-American in 1926.

The Michigan football team takes direction on the practice field during the 1926 season.

Fielding Yost inspects the box-seat area of the new stadium. As the athletic director, beginning in 1921, he was in charge of more than just the football team and insisted on being involved in every aspect of the building of the stadium. With its completion, Michigan football passed into a new era.

Fielding Yost's hard work and dedication to improving athletics at Michigan included his role in the building of Michigan Stadium. His position as athletic director at the university allowed him to push for such improvements. Here on the day of the stadium's dedication, October 22, 1927, Yost is surrounded by the nearly 85,000 spectators who witnessed Michigan's 21–0 victory over Ohio State.

# THE KIPKE-CRISLER YEARS

## (1927–1947)

Yost acquired two live wolverines that were brought to all the big games for a year and are seen here at the stadium dedication game. Named "Bennie" and "Biff," the two wolverines lived in a small zoo near the natural science museum, but their behavior became too violent and they were later moved to the Detroit Zoo.

During the 1927 stadium dedication game, an Ohio State player stiff-arms a Michigan defender. Michigan's 21–0 victory was its last over Ohio State until 1930.

A former player who assisted under Fielding Yost, Elton Wieman took over as head coach of the Wolverines in 1927. Seen here at a team practice, Wieman coached only two seasons at Michigan but later experienced great success at Princeton.

This aerial view shows Michigan Stadium packed for the Harvard game of 1929. In their most recent meeting, at Harvard in 1914, Michigan lost 7–0. But in Ann Arbor in 1929, Michigan defeated Harvard, though it was a close game, 14–12.

With rising-star players such as Gerald Ford (48) and Willis Ward (61), Michigan's 1932 football team completed a perfect season, winning all of its matches and becoming national champions. Coach Harry Kipke's style of play favored the offensive attack.

Willis Ward was the second African-American to earn a varsity letter playing football at the University of Michigan; George Jewett was the first, in 1890. Originally a track star, Ward was recruited by Coach Kipke, and his outstanding play helped the 1932 squad to its undefeated season. Ward experienced prejudice in the lead-up to a 1934 game, however, when Georgia Tech threatened not to play if Ward was allowed on the field. This enraged the Michigan team, but in the end Ward was not permitted to participate.

Dedicated in 1923, the Yost Field House was named in honor of football coach and athletic director Fielding Yost, seen here walking in front of the sports facility in 1938.

Michigan coach Fritz Crisler talks with team captain Fred Janke during a practice in 1938. Crisler was brought over from Princeton University, where he had done excellent work. At the University of Chicago, Crisler played football under Amos Alonzo Stagg and earned nine varsity letters in three sports.

The Michigan coaching staff of 1938 poses for a field-level photo. Left to right are Wally Weber, Clarence Munn, Fritz Crisler, Bennie Oosterbaan, Campbell Dickson, and Earl Martineau.

Michigan's Tom Harmon follows the lead block around end against Illinois in 1938. An All-American at halfback, Harmon became the first Michigan player to win the Heisman Trophy when he was chosen after the 1940 season.

In the 1938 season, Michigan fullback Howard Mehaffey (22) reportedly had his nose broken 13 times, usually because he hit his opponents head-first and hard. Yet a broken nose couldn't slow him down; after every injury he kept on playing with a nose guard.

The University of Michigan's defense makes a key stop against Pennsylvania during their 1938 meeting, a 19–13 victory for the Wolverines.

Few plays in football are as exciting as an interception made on an attempted touchdown pass. Here Tom Harmon intercepts Nile Kinnick during the Iowa game in 1939. Harmon had another spectacular interception on Michigan's five-yard line and returned it 95 yards for a touchdown. Harmon scored four touchdowns and kicked three extra points in the defeat of Iowa.

Homecoming decorations were typically designed by the different fraternities and sororities on campus. This one from 1939 worked a *Gulliver's Travels* theme.

The versatility of Tom Harmon on the field was astounding; besides playing both ways, offense and defense, he was an excellent placekicker and is seen here kicking an extra point against Ohio State in 1939. Harmon kicked 33 extra points overall during his three-season Michigan career.

Tom Harmon and Forest Evashevski, posing over a typewriter, worked well together on and off the field. They were close friends and important players in Crisler's single-wing system, which was designed for the quarterback to block for the running back. The system worked perfectly with Harmon's speed and Evashevski's blocking ability.

Tom Harmon, wearing his familiar number 98, scored 33 touchdowns and rushed for 2,134 yards during the three seasons he played at Michigan. Forest Evashevski may have been the quarterback, but that didn't stop Harmon from throwing 16 touchdown passes.

The Michigan backs of 1940 see how high they can throw a football. Seen from left to right, Dave Nelson, Norm Call, Cliff Wise, Tom Harmon, Forest Evashevski, and Bob Westfall had much collective experience under their belts as they prepared for the season. Michigan took second place in the conference, the team's only loss being by one point to Minnesota.

Tom Harmon runs the ball against Michigan State College (later Michigan State University) in 1940. Harmon won the Maxwell and Walter Camp trophies, in addition to the Heisman, while at Michigan.

The Wolverines' defense takes down a Pennsylvania player in their 1940 meeting. In this era, most players, including Tom Harmon, played both offense and defense.

The first plane trip made by a Michigan football team was in 1940 to play the University of California. United Airlines painted on the side of the airplane: "Michigan Football Special."

Albert Wistert (11) followed in his brother Francis's footsteps at the University of Michigan, playing left tackle. Here against Ohio State in 1941, Wistert leads the blocking as Tom Kuzma scores Michigan's first touchdown in a game that would end in a 20–20 tie.

Fritz Crisler leans on a car on the practice field while talking with the captain and quarterback of his 1942 team, George Ceithaml (holding the football); Bennie Oosterbaan, one of Crisler's assistant coaches; and Albert Wistert, his All-American tackle.

Legendary University of Michigan football equipment manager Henry Hatch works on three jerseys. His care not only for the equipment used by the Michigan team but also for the players was in part responsible for his posthumous induction into Michigan's Hall of Honor in 1992.

Four former Michigan students in pilot school at the Greenwood, Mississippi, Army Air Field listen to a radio broadcast of the Michigan vs. Ohio State game in 1943. Among the many young athletes who lent their skills to the war effort, several came back after the war to play college football at Michigan.

Michigan's Ed McNeill (85) runs under a pass during the 1946 Army game, which Michigan lost 20–13.

Coach Fritz Crisler stands near the 50-yard line watching his team in 1947. He used different personnel for the two lines, offensive and defensive, and only Bump Elliott and Jack Weisenburger played both ways. Crisler's playbook consisted of crisscrosses, spins, reverse laterals, and quick hits that made it hard to know who had the ball, but the Michigan players knew what they were doing and dominated their opponents.

The Michigan Wolverines prepare to leave for Pasadena, California, for the 1948 Rose Bowl game against the University of Southern California Trojans. Michigan's 49–0 thrashing of USC proved to be more than just a postseason victory; it allowed Michigan to vault to first place in the Associated Press national rankings after trailing top-ranked Notre Dame by one spot at the close of the regular season.

On the practice field before the Rose Bowl, Fritz Crisler speaks to his Wolverines. Crisler's 1947 team was a winning machine, completing a perfect season and extending that undefeated run through the Rose Bowl on New Year's Day 1948. Michigan's 49–0 Rose Bowl victory matched exactly that of the 1901 team led by Fielding Yost. With All-Americans Bob Chappuis and Bump Elliott at halfback, the 1947 Michigan team was unstoppable.

# STAR PLAYERS TURN COACH

## (1948–1968)

Michigan's marching band sits for dinner en route to the 1948 Rose Bowl game in Pasadena, California. On this trip the band became the first ever from the Big Ten to travel and play at the Rose Bowl. When, later, the 1950 edition of the Michigan band performed at both the Rose Bowl and Yankee Stadium, it was given the nickname "Transcontinental Marching Band."

The Minnesota Gophers challenge Michigan's defense in this action from 1948. Al Wahl (72) and Dick Kempthorn (38) are among the Michigan tacklers. The defense held the Gophers to only 14 points as Michigan went on to win its sixth game of a perfect season.

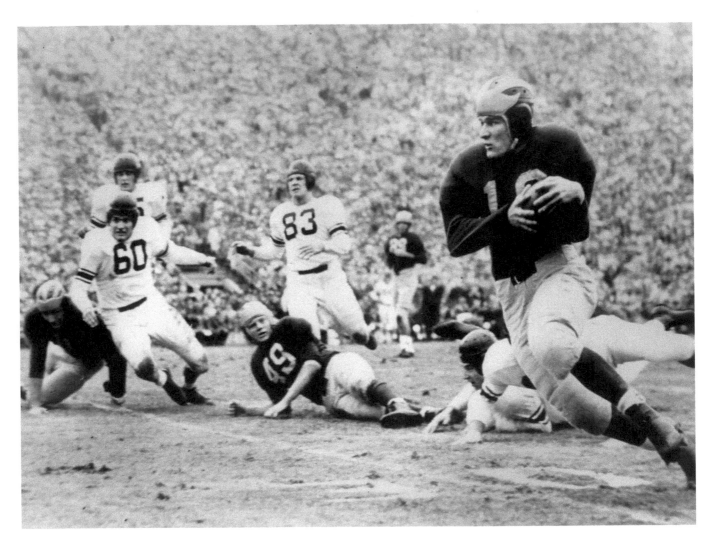

Michigan halfback Leo Koceski carries the ball around left end against Minnesota while fellow halfback Chuck Ortmann (49) looks on after blocking. Koceski's outstanding play was recognized by his teammates when they awarded him the 1948 Meyer Morton Award, given each year after spring practice to the player who shows the most promise. Named for an alumnus, the award was established by the M Club in 1925.

Michigan halfback Leo Koceski (18) strove to be a triple-threat player like his hero Tom Harmon—able to run, pass, and kick with skill. Here he blocks while Chuck Ortmann runs the ball upfield in Michigan's 1948 victory over Illinois.

The previous year's Meyer Morton Award winner, Leo Koceski carries the ball for Michigan during a game in 1949.

Pete Elliott was a letter winner in three sports—golf, basketball, and football. The only Michigan athlete to earn twelve letters, he played on four national championship teams—one in basketball, one in golf, and the 1947 and 1948 football teams.

An Ohio State player leans forward for minimal yardage against the Wolverines in the infamous "Snow Bowl" of 1950. Michigan had traveled to Ohio State to once again play a game to decide the Big Ten championship, but the blizzard conditions were so harsh the spectators could barely see the field, and the players had a difficult time gaining their footing, let alone yards. Still, Michigan managed a 9–3 victory that sent them to sunny Pasadena.

Louis Elbel, composer of "The Victors," conducts the Michigan Marching Band at halftime of a game during the 1952 season—54 years after he wrote the famous Michigan fight song.

Michigan went into the 1953 Ohio State game following two losses in which the Wolverines could muster only nine points total. Yet Michigan put up 20 against Ohio State while holding the Buckeyes scoreless. Center John Morrow (55) and halfback Ted Kress (41) were among the Michigan players who left the stadium that day with heads held high.

By 1955, the time of this scene, Michigan football paraphernalia was commonly sold on the street outside the stadium on game day.

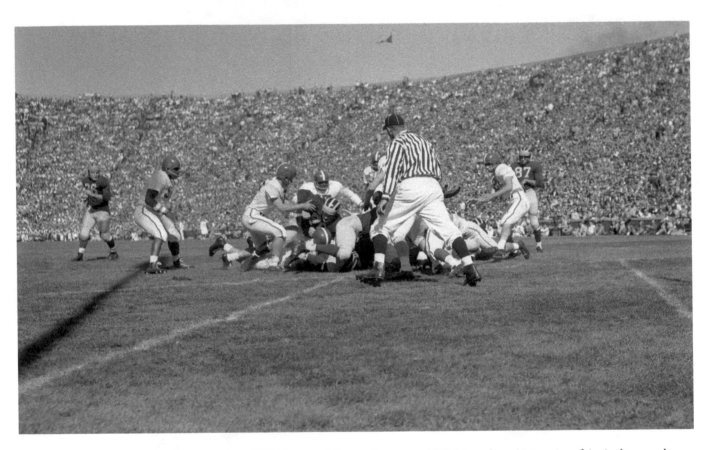

The in-state rivalry between the University of Michigan and the newly renamed Michigan State University of Agriculture and Applied Science produced a close game here in 1955, with Michigan winning 14–7. Eight years later, the "Agriculture and Applied Science" part of Michigan State's name would be dropped.

Michigan halfback Jim Pace runs the ball over a path cleared in the 1955 Army game. Pace scored the last touchdown in the 26–2 Michigan victory, while teammate Terry Barr returned a punt 82 yards for an earlier touchdown. Army scored its only two points off a safety in the last seconds of the game.

Tony Branoff (17), the 1955 Michigan team's starting right halfback, runs the ball against Army alongside guard Charles Krahnke (62). Before this Michigan victory, Army had dominated their encounters for a decade.

Even though Ron Kramer blocked this Michigan State punt, Michigan still lost to their in-state rivals in 1956 by a 9–0 shutout. Several Michigan scoring efforts fell short, including a 27-yard field goal attempt by Kramer that veered left. The Spartans' rain-soaked victory held the Michigan crowd in silence.

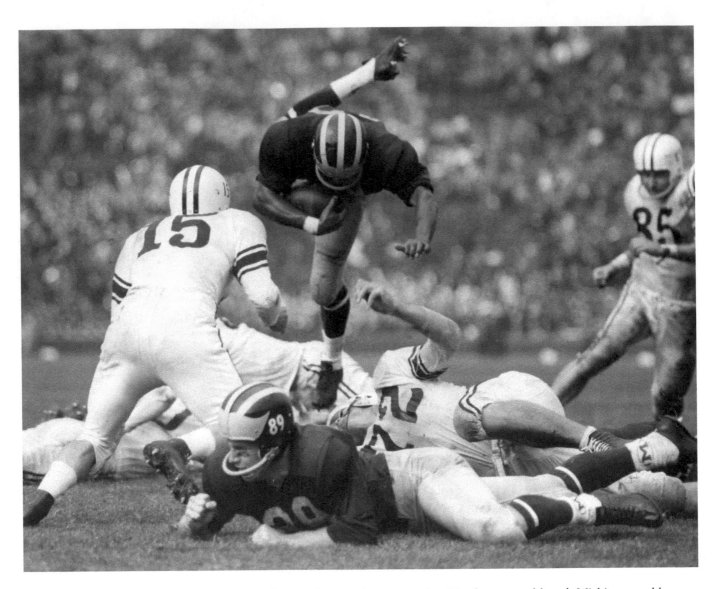

An attempted touchdown leap by Jim Pace fell short in the second quarter against Northwestern, although Michigan would score on the next play. Beginning with this 1956 game the ticket rules were changed: a University of Michigan ID was now required in order for a ticketholder to sit in the student section, due to the number of tickets sold on the street at previous games.

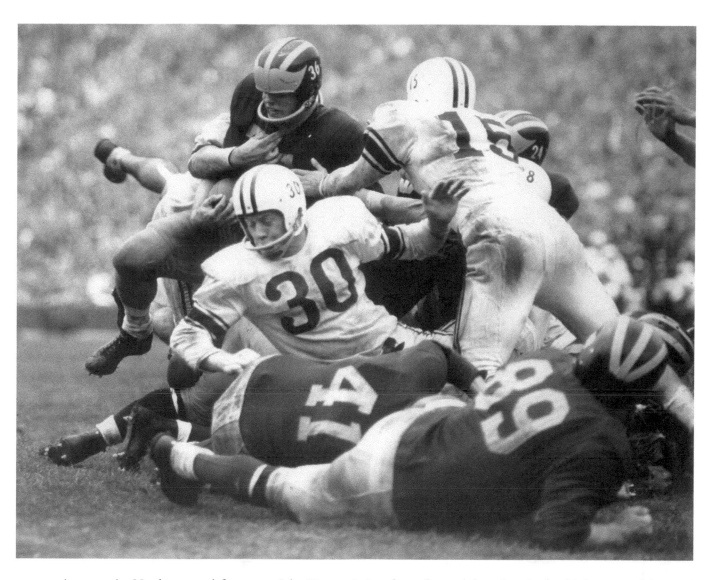

An aggressive Northwestern defense stops John Herrnstein just short of a touchdown here in the third quarter of the 1956 game, but Michigan's overall dominance would lead to a victory. Herrnstein's father, William, and an uncle had both played for Michigan, and his grandfather Albert Herrnstein played under Yost in 1901-2.

Ron Kramer (87) appeared on the Ed Sullivan television show in 1956 as a member of the All-American football team. Following his Michigan career he played professionally for the Green Bay Packers under legendary coach Vince Lombardi. Later traded to the Detroit Lions, he finally retired from football in 1968.

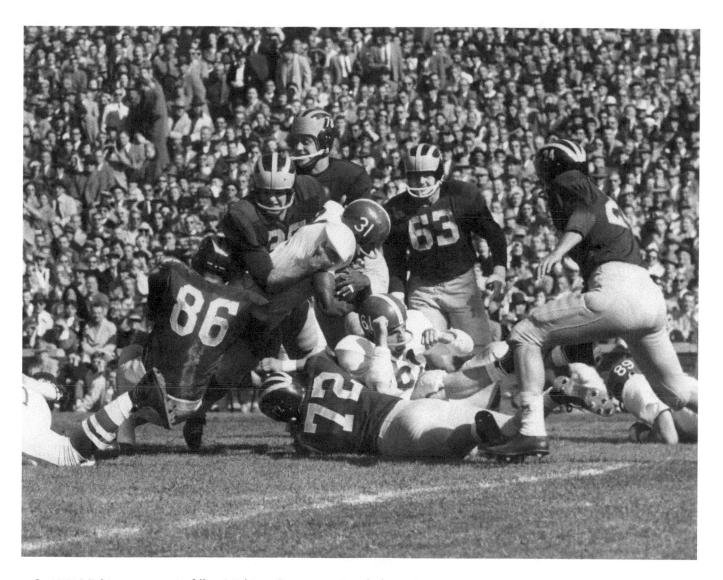

In 1957 Michigan once again fell to Michigan State. Even though the Wolverines' defense fought hard, they were unable to stop the Spartans, who outscored Michigan 35–6. The in-state rivalry continues to this day, as the two schools located only 60 minutes from each other battle every year for the Paul Bunyan Trophy.

Against Indiana the following season, 1958, Michigan was not as fortunate, losing by two points, 8–6. Here coach Bennie Oosterbaan stands on the sidelines with his rain-drenched team. This was Oosterbaan's last season as head coach. He closed his Michigan career with a record of 63-33-4.

Michigan's new head coach, Chalmers "Bump" Elliott, poses with his 1959 staff. Left to right are Elliott, Don Dufek, Henry Fonde, Jack Nelson, Bob Hollway, and Jack Fouts. Elliott, Fonde, Hollway, and Dufek had all been University of Michigan football players.

Also taking place during the 1962 homecoming festivities was a twist contest the day before the Minnesota game. One hundred contestants twisted to the music of the Road Runners Band. The winners were chosen from 20 finalists.

The Michigan bench at the 1965 Rose Bowl sees congratulations all around as the Wolverines beat the Oregon State Ducks, 34–7. Mel Anthony scored the first touchdown on an 84-yard run from scrimmage. His three touchdowns tied a bowl record then held by fellow Wolverine Jack Weisenburger.

Left halfback Jim Detwiler, in his first game back from an injury, carries the football against Georgia in 1965. This was Michigan's first loss of the season and would be followed by three more before a win against Wisconsin.

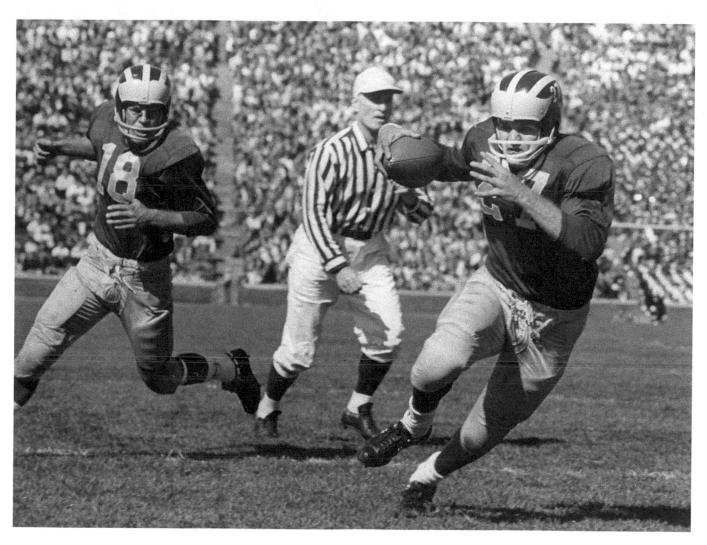

Dick Vidmer (27), the starting quarterback of the 1966 Michigan team, completed 117 passes for 1,609 yards. Fullback Dick Sygar (18) doubled at safety and was thus part of Michigan's last line of defense. Michigan ended the season with a record of 6-4.

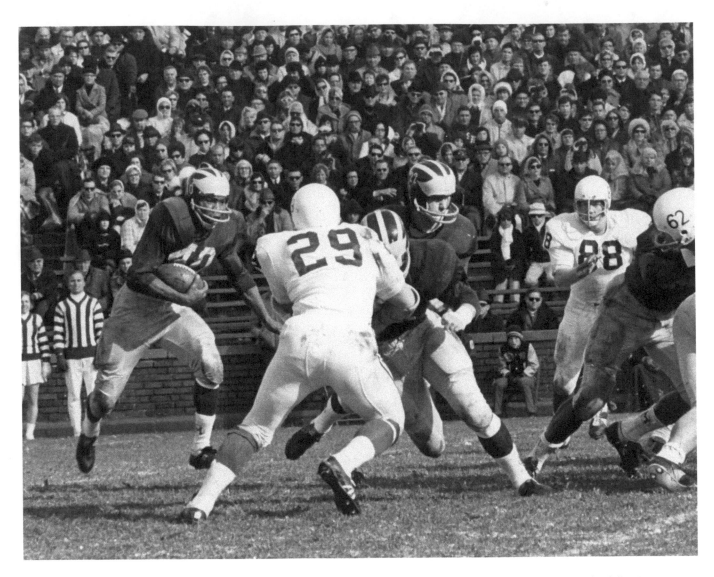

Halfback Ron Johnson (40) gained 167 yards rushing for Michigan in this 1967 victory over Northwestern. The following season he was voted All-American and broke numerous school rushing records. He ran for 347 yards in a 1968 game against Wisconsin and won the *Chicago Tribune*'s Silver Football as the most valuable player in the Big Ten Conference.

# THE BO ERA BEGINS

## (1969–1979)

Heading into the 1969 season, Michigan hired new head coach Bo Schembechler, seen at left, to lead them into the next decade of Michigan football. Joining the new coach here at the press conference announcing his appointment are athletic director Don Canham, at center, and Bump Elliott.

Bo Schembechler supervises a Michigan practice in 1969, his first year as head coach.

Schembechler speaks to his team during practice. Always able to inspire his players, he would make such statements as "I don't need to tell you talent is important—anyone knows that—but it's easy to get blindsided by it. And it's a big mistake, too. Character counts for more. Much more."

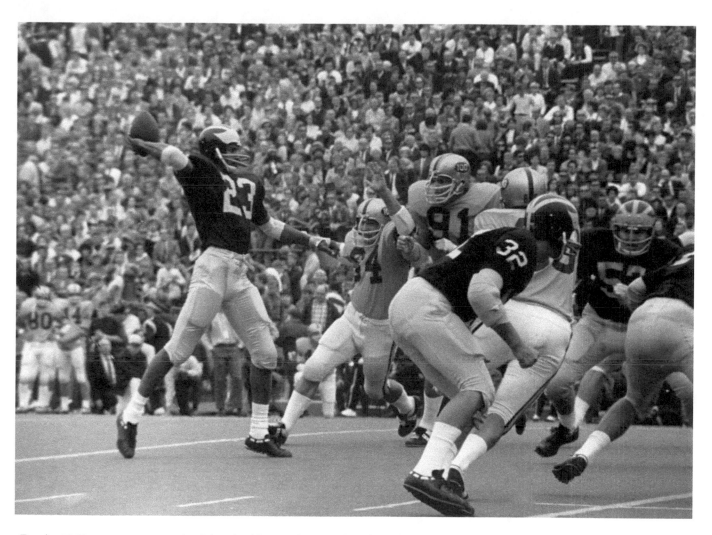

For the 1969 season opener under Schembechler, Michigan defeated Vanderbilt 42–14. Here backup quarterback Jim Betts passes over the Vanderbilt line.

William Revelli, also known as the "Chief," conducts the Michigan Marching Band at Michigan Stadium, as he did regularly from 1935 until 1971. Under Revelli's direction the marching band grew and so did the music department, which the university took over in 1940. He didn't only teach music; he inspired future music teachers.

Michigan tackle Jack Harpring (71), winner of the team's 1969 Frederick Matthaei Award for athletic and academic achievement, blocks for John Gabler (18) during the Purdue game. Gabler gained valuable yards rushing and receiving to help push Michigan past Purdue.

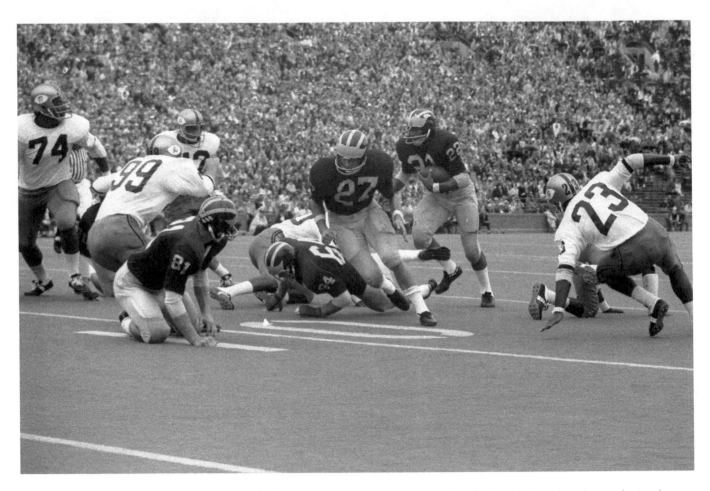

Taking his turn at blocking, Michigan quarterback Don Moorhead clears a path for halfback Glen Doughty during the Purdue game. Michigan had difficulty getting down the field as penalty flags were being dropped everywhere. The Wolverines still managed a win against the aggressive Boilermakers, who knocked safety Tom Curtis out cold in the fourth quarter.

The University of Michigan's 1969 homecoming parade took place before the Wisconsin game. Here paraders travel down State Street toward the stadium to cheer on the Wolverines.

Bo Schembechler greets his mentor-turned-rival Woody Hayes, under whom he served as an assistant for five years at Ohio State. Their first time matching wits in the Michigan vs. Ohio State game was a classic that would make the famous rivalry even more meaningful. The outcome of this annual game would determine the Big Ten championship year after year.

Michigan defensive back Barry Pierson tucks the ball tight during a 60-yard punt return that set up the final touchdown against Ohio State. Blocking for Pierson is Bruce Elliott (21). Pierson also had three interceptions to go with five tackles. His return, followed by a yard gain by Garvie Craw, would allow Don Moorhead to fake a pitch wide and go in for the touchdown.

The sideline celebration was well worth the wait as Michigan stopped Ohio State's 22-game winning streak. The 1969 game was monumental as more than just a victory over the number one team in the conference. Tom Curtis set an NCAA record for career interception-return yardage when his two interceptions that day gave him 431 return yards as a Wolverine.

Morris Abrams (73) lifts two roses toward the fans, signifying that Michigan had just tied Ohio State for the Big Ten Conference title and was therefore going to the Rose Bowl.

Schembechler leads his team onto the field for picture day 1970. After beating Ohio State to earn the 1969 conference co-championship, the 1970 Wolverines were prepared to win, and win they did. Schembechler did more than lead his team onto the field, he led them to a nearly perfect season. On the eve of the 1970 Ohio State game, he found himself in Hayes's place of the year before—undefeated. But a 20–9 loss to Hayes's team left Michigan tied for second place in the conference, and the rival Buckeyes took the championship.

The team was getting used to seeing Schembechler on the practice field doing more than just coaching with a clipboard. As a former player for Miami University of Ohio, he liked to demonstrate plays to make sure his team understood exactly what was needed.

With his strength and skills, Dan Dierdorf, a 1970 All-American, was considered one of the greatest offensive linemen ever to play for Michigan. He went on to star professionally with the St. Louis Cardinals of the NFL and was eventually elected to the Pro Football Hall of Fame.

Left tackle Reggie McKenzie (65) protects Don Moorhead (27) as he moves about the pocket looking for a receiver against Texas A&M in 1970. Moorhead completed only three passes, overthrowing Paul Staroba more than once in the 14–10 Michigan victory. The offense may have struggled at the beginning of the season, but it would soon be putting up many more points per game than it did against the hard-hitting Aggies.

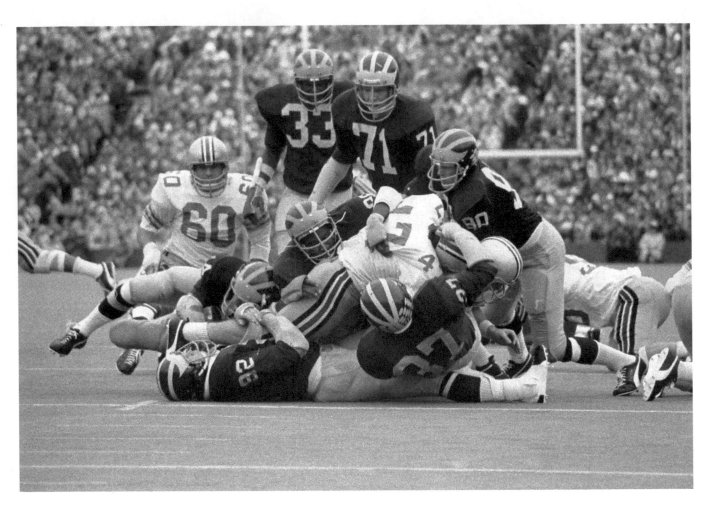

David Gallagher (71) and Michael Taylor (33) stand at the ready as their Michigan teammates stop Ohio State's Elmer Lippert in the 1971 matchup. With a 10–7 victory, Michigan would complete an undefeated regular season and take the conference, but would then lose the Rose Bowl to Stanford by a single point. Michigan was unable to win it for Schembechler, who had been unable to attend their Rose Bowl after the 1969 season due to a heart attack on the eve of the event.

Congressman Gerald Ford visits his alma mater in 1972 and attends a Michigan football practice—a setting he knew well as a former player under Harry Kipke. Little could anyone know that a year after this visit he would become the first vice president to hold office under the terms of the 25th Amendment, and that he would subsequently become the 38th president of the United States.

The Michigan football team huddles around Schembechler during the 1973 season, which saw the Wolverines continue their success with a tie for the conference championship. With words that could inspire any athlete, Schembechler said in one of his famous talks that "nothing, not even your greatest star, can come before the team. The team. The team. Because when you've got that, you've got something special."

In line with long tradition, the 1973 University of Michigan cheerleaders perform one of their stunts. The troupe was all male until 1974, when women were finally admitted into the cheerleading program.

Bo Schembechler speaks with quarterback Dennis Franklin (9) during the 1973 Ohio State game. Franklin scored Michigan's only touchdown with a 10-yard run on fourth down. He broke his collarbone in the final quarter of the game, an apparent factor in the Big Ten's decision that Ohio State would represent the conference in the Rose Bowl. During Franklin's 1972-74 career as Michigan's quarterback he was unable to beat the Buckeyes or play in the Rose Bowl.

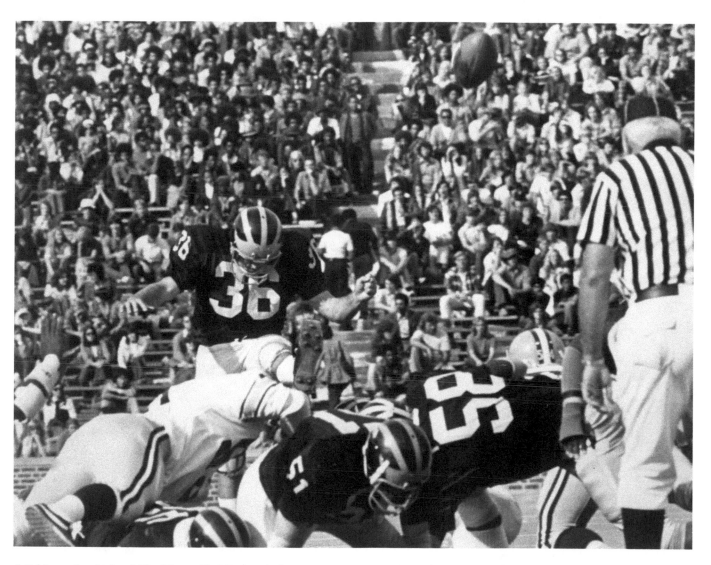

Michigan placekicker Mike "Super Toe" Lantry (36) attempts to score against Ohio State. He hit a 30-yard field goal in the fourth quarter that, coupled with Franklin's touchdown, brought the Wolverines back level with the Buckeyes. Lantry had two more chances to score: a 58-yard field goal attempt that just missed to the left, and—with 28 seconds remaining—a 44-yard attempt that sailed right.

Michigan prepares to take on Navy in the 1974 matchup at Michigan Stadium. Captains Dennis Franklin and David Brown jump up and tap the banner for luck—which they didn't need in a 52–0 win.

Michigan's Jim Pickens (18), Richard Koschalk (92), Rex Mackall (49), Dan Jilek (81), and Jim Bolden (22) rush the Missouri punter during Michigan's 34–7 victory of 1975.

Members of the 1925 Michigan football team reunite for the 1975 homecoming game against Indiana. The 1925 team lost only one game, to Northwestern, and gave up only three points the entire season. Left to right are George Babcock, Sam Babcock, Bob Brown (the captain), Sid Dewey, Bill Flora, Benny Friedman, Fred Fuller, Charles Grube, Louie Gilbert, George Hawkins, Bennie Oosterbaan, Fred Parker, and Dutch Stamman.

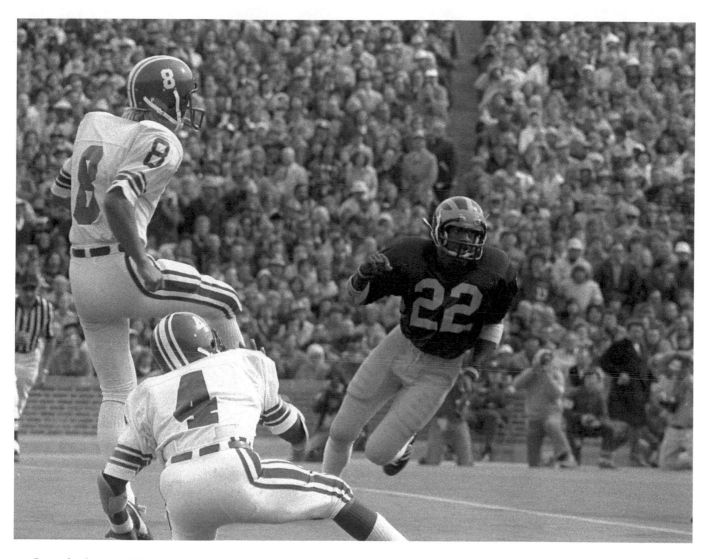

Cornerback Jim Bolden (22) of the 1976 Michigan team attempts to block a Michigan State kick. The final score was 42–10 in favor of the Wolverines, as they attacked the rival Spartans from the outset. This was Schembechler's 71st victory, tying him with Fritz Crisler for career wins.

A team captain and All-American, running back Rob Lytle (41) scored the final touchdown against Ohio State in 1976. The Wolverines completely shut down the Buckeyes 22–0, making the two teams Big Ten co-champions once again but this time with Michigan going to the Rose Bowl. Lytle finished his senior year with 1,469 yards rushing on the season and 3,317 yards for his career, both school records at the time.

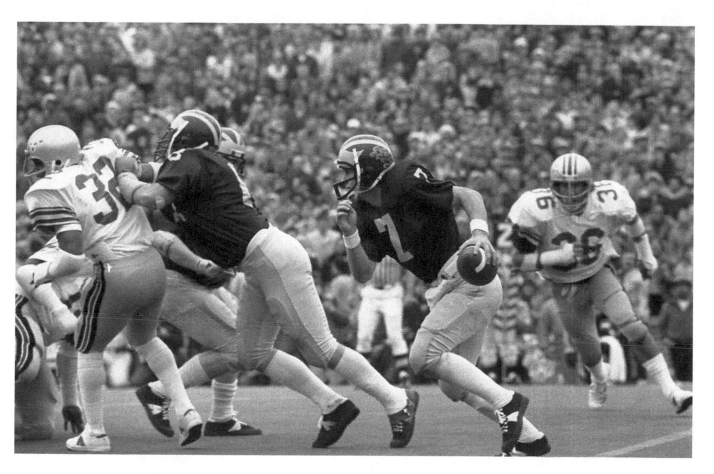

Quarterback Rick Leach (7) scored one of two touchdowns against Ohio State in 1977 in another Michigan victory over its archrival. Leach, a left-hander, broke Michigan records of the day for career total offense and touchdowns and the season record for touchdown passes, and set an NCAA record for most touchdowns accounted for, with 82. He was an All-American for the Michigan baseball team as well.

Bo Schembechler makes sure Michigan quarterback Rick Leach understands him on the sidelines during the 1978 Purdue game. Leach was voted the team's most valuable player that year as well as the Big Ten's.

In his last showdown with Ohio State, in 1978, Leach did his part to make sure his team left the field as victors. Seen here throwing a touchdown pass, he helped send Michigan to the Rose Bowl.

The future looked promising as two freshman players, Ed Murnasky (72) and Mark Warth (60), carried Schembechler off the field in 1978 after beating Ohio State, just like his 1969 team had done.

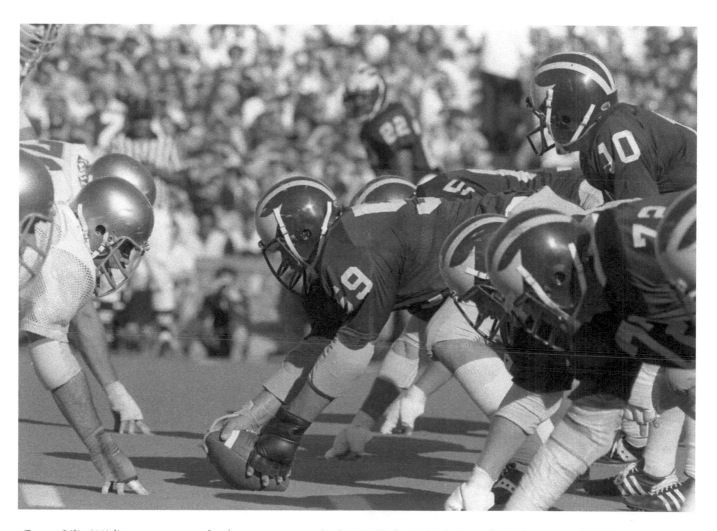

George Lilja (59) lines up at center for the snap to quarterback B. J. Dickey (10) during a 49–7 victory over Northwestern to start the Wolverines' 1979 season.

B. J. Dickey looks upfield in this action from the 1979 Notre Dame game, which Michigan lost 12–10.

Butch Woolfolk (24) lifts teammate Anthony Carter in the air after the dramatic, final-seconds score that gave Michigan its 1979 win over Indiana. Carter was a three-time All-American. Michigan may not have won a championship that year, but the amazing win over Indiana lives on.

# Notes on the Photographs

These notes, listed by page number, attempt to include all aspects known of the photographs. Each of the photographs is identified by the page number, a title or description, photographer and collection, archive, and call or box number when applicable. Although every attempt was made to collect all data, in some cases complete data may have been unavailable due to the age and condition of some of the photographs and records.

Printed in the USA
CPSIA information can be obtained
at www.ICGtesting.com
JSHW072022140824
68134JS00042B/3748

9 781683 369004